My Five Super Senses
I HEAR IT!

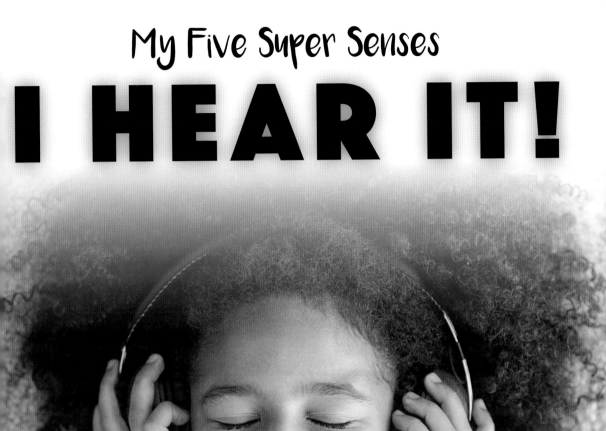

Theresa Emminizer

PowerKiDS
press

T0014647

My Five Super Senses
I HEAR IT!

Theresa Emminizer

PK Beginners

I use my ears to hear things!

I hear my brother sing.
It's loud!

I hear my cat meow.
It's quiet.

I hear the bird. Cheep!

I hear the rain.

Drip, drop!

I hear the leaves
under my feet.

I hear my friend's voice.

I hear my bike bell.
It rings!

17

I hear the water. Splash!

I hear my dog.
Yap, yap!

There are so many things to hear!

Published in 2024 by The Rosen Publishing Group, Inc.
2544 Clinton Street, Buffalo, NY 14224

First Edition

Editor: Theresa Emminizer
Book Design: Rachel Rising

Photo Credits: Cover, p.1 Africa Studio/Shutterstock.com; p. 3 Anatoliy Karlyuk/Shutterstock.com; p. 5 Prostock-studio/Shutterstock.com; p. 7 LightField Studios/Shutterstock.com; p. 9 mikumistock/Shutterstock.com; p. 11 Tatyana Vyc/Shutterstock.com; p. 13 Ekaterina Pokrovsky/Shutterstock.com; p. 15 PeopleImages.com - Yuri A/Shutterstock.com; p. 17 H.Tuller/Shutterstock.com; p. 19 stocknadia/Shutterstock.co; p. 21 Nicky J Graham/Shutterstock.com; p. 23 Sunny studio/Shutterstock.com.

Library of Congress Cataloging-in-Publication Data

Names: Emminizer, Theresa, author.
Title: I hear it! / Theresa Emminizer.
Description: [Buffalo, NY] : PowerKids Press, [2023] | Series: My five
    super senses | Audience: Grades K-1
Identifiers: LCCN 2023033264 (print) | LCCN 2023033265 (ebook) | ISBN
    9781499443325 (library binding) | ISBN 9781499443318 (paperback) | ISBN
    9781499443332 (ebook)
Subjects: LCSH: Hearing–Juvenile literature. | Senses and
    sensation–Juvenile literature.
Classification: LCC QP462.2 .E56 2023 (print) | LCC QP462.2 (ebook) | DDC
    612.8/5–dc23/eng/20230726
LC record available at https://lccn.loc.gov/2023033264
LC ebook record available at https://lccn.loc.gov/2023033265

Manufactured in the United States of America

CPSIA Compliance Information: Batch #CWPK24. For further information contact Rosen Publishing at 1-800-237-9932.

Find us on